MONEY MATH

KATIE MARSICO

Lerner Publications ◆ Minneapolis

To Nico Filice—one of the bravest boys I know

Lerner Publications Company
A division of Lerner Publishing Group, Inc.
241 First Avenue North
Minneapolis, MN 55401 USA

For reading levels and more information, look up this title at www.lernerbooks.com.

Photo Acknowledgments
The images in this book are used with the permission of: © iStockphoto.com/babyblueut, p. 1; © iStockphoto.com/emyerson, p. 4; © Laura Westlund/Independent Picture Service, pp. 5 (top); 13, 25 (bottom), 31; © iStockphoto.com/alubalish, pp. 5, 7, 11, 15, 19, 23 (torn paper); © iStockphoto.com/spxChrome, pp. 5, 7, 11, 13, 17, 19, 25, 27 (notebook background); © iStockphoto.com/ParkerDeen, p. 6; © iStockphoto.com/mbbirdy, p. 7; © Echo/Cultura/Getty Images, p. 8; © iStockphoto.com/AnikaSalsera, p. 9; © Alina Vincent Photography, LLC/E+/Getty Images, p. 10; © Brand X Pictures/Stockbyte/Getty Images, p. 11; © Rob Lewine//Getty Images, p. 12; © iStockphoto.com/klosfoto, p. 13; Megan Maloy Image Source/Newscom, p. 14; © iStockphoto.com/richcarey, p. 15; © Tom Merton/OJO Images/Getty Images, p. 16; © Robyn Mackenzie/Dreamstime.com, p. 17; Jose Luis Pelaez Inc Blend Images/Newscom, p. 18; © rCarner/Shutterstock.com, p. 19; © Michael Wheatley/Alamy, p. 20; © iStockphoto.com/Becart, p. 21; © iStockphoto.com/monkeybusinessimages, p. 22; © iStockphoto.com/DebbiSmirnoff, p. 23; © Comstock Images/Stockbyte/Getty Images, p. 24; © iStockphoto.com/unalozmen, p. 25 (top); © Martin Barraud/Caiaimage/Getty Images, p. 26; United States Treasury, p. 27; © iStockphoto.com/kali9, p. 28; © Todd Strand/Independent Picture Service, p. 29; © iStockphoto.com/rusm, (grid background throughout).

Front cover: © Donald P Oehman/Shutterstock.com. Back cover: © iStockphoto.com/robynmac.

Main body text set in Conduit ITC Std 14/18. Typeface provided by International Typeface Corp.

Library of Congress Cataloging-in-Publication Data

Marsico, Katie, 1980– author.
    Money math / by Katie Marsico.
        pages cm. — (Math everywhere!)
    Audience: Ages 8–10
    Audience: K to grade 3
    ISBN 978-1-4677-8579-2 (lb : alk. paper) — ISBN 978-1-4677-8632-4 (pb : alk. paper) —
ISBN 978-1-4677-8633-1 (eb pdf)
    1. Mathematics—Juvenile literature. 2. Money-making projects for children—Juvenile literature. 3. Word problems (Mathematics)—Juvenile literature. I. Title. II. Series: Marsico, Katie, 1980– Math everywhere!
QA40.5.M3774 2016
513.2—dc23   2014046761

Manufactured in the United States of America
1 – CG – 7/15/15

TABLE OF CONTENTS

A CLOSER LOOK AT ALLOWANCE

Clink! Ah, there's nothing like the sound of coins clanging together in a piggy bank. Or perhaps you put all your cash in a savings account. Either way, you probably use math to manage your money. Math skills help people make smart financial decisions. Need proof? Start by taking a look at your allowance!

That's what Marge and her parents do at the end of the month. Mom and Dad pay Marge, who is ten, a monthly allowance of $3 for every year of her age. To earn her allowance, she's expected to help with certain chores around the house.

On Tuesdays and Thursdays, Marge is responsible for loading the dishwasher. On weekends, she's supposed to walk the family dog after breakfast. Finally, she needs to take out the trash on Mondays, Wednesdays, and Fridays.

Marge and her parents keep a chore chart to track her progress. If she forgets to do a chore, Mom and Dad deduct $1 from her monthly allowance.

Today is the last day of the month—time to calculate Marge's earnings! Together, she and her parents check out the chore chart below. **How much money should Marge expect to get this month?**

Marge's Monthly Chore Chart

	Sunday (dog)	Monday (trash)	Tuesday (dishes)	Wednesday (trash)	Thursday (dishes)	Friday (trash)	Saturday (dog)
Week 1	😊	😧	😊	😊	😊	😊	😊
Week 2	😊	😧	😊	😊	😊	😧	😊
Week 3	😊	😊	😊	😊	😊	😧	😊
Week 4	😊	😊	😊	😊	😊	😊	😊
Week 5	😊	😧					

😊 Chore successfully completed 　 😧 Chore not successfully completed 　 ▢ First/last days of the month

DO THE MATH!

Suppose you're ten years old and your parents are trying to figure out how much of an allowance to pay you. Mom's thinking $25 per month. But Dad suggests 50¢ a week for each year of your age. You know there are 52 weeks in a year. What's the better deal? Will that change when you reach a certain age? Why?

Check your answers to all questions on pages 30–31.

SHOVEL, SAVE, SHOP!

Snow is an important part of winter fun. For Joel, it's also an important way to add to his savings! Whenever flakes start falling, he and his brother, Jeff, are ready with their shovels.

Their neighbors pay them between $10 and $20 to clear their walkways. Mr. Jacobs, the Smiths, and the Peñas each pay $10. Mr. Thomas's walkway is a bit longer, so he pays $15. Finally, the Browns and the Mitchells each pay $20. That's because they get part of their driveways shoveled too.

This winter, Joel is hoping to earn enough money to buy a new pair of skis. They're $149.95. So far, he has $18.50 saved in his sock drawer. Joel also has $56 in a savings account at a local bank.

Friday night, a blizzard blows through town. On Saturday morning, Joel and Jeff get busy! Joel shovels for the Smiths, Mr. Thomas, and the Browns. Jeff takes care of Mr. Jacobs and the Mitchells.

Sometimes Joel shovels for more houses than Jeff. Sometimes it's the other way around. The boys don't mind, since it always seems to even out by the end of winter. Yet Jeff also knows Joel is saving up for new skis. So he offers to let him take the Peñas' walkway. **Should Joel accept, or has he already earned enough money?**

DO THE MATH!

Let's say you're saving up for the same skis as Joel. So far, you have $113.15 in the bank. Your neighbor offers to let you shovel her driveway for $15 each time it snows. How many times will it have to snow before you earn enough for your skis? (Round up to the nearest whole number.)

BILLS FOR BOTTLES

Bess knows that recycling is good for the environment—and a good way to earn some extra money! The last Saturday of every month, Bess's sister Jane sorts through the recycling bin. She collects all the aluminum cans and the plastic and glass containers. Then Jane and Dad take these items to the recycling center.

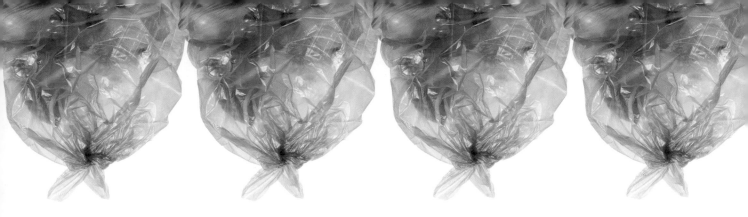

Usually, the center pays per pound for different recyclable items. Sometimes, however, Jane only has a small amount of aluminum, glass, or plastic. Then the center pays per item. The usual rate is 5¢ for each container that holds less than 24 fluid ounces (710 milliliters). For anything larger, the rate is 10¢ per container.

Jane usually cleans and sorts items the night before taking them in. But this Friday, Jane is going to a birthday party. So she asks Bess to help her clean and sort the recyclables. In return, Jane will give her 50 percent of whatever she earns Saturday.

The deal sounds good to Bess! As Bess is sorting, she finds three aluminum cans to add to this month's collection. Each one holds 12 fluid ounces (355 ml).

When Jane returns from the recycling center on Saturday, she says they made $5.35. Since they only had a little aluminum, the center paid her per container. Jane tells Bess she'll give her 100 percent of the profit for her three cans. She also owes her 50 percent of everything else they earned. **How much money should Bess get?**

DECIDE WHAT TO DEPOSIT

Hmmm...savings account or spending money? That's the big question Rob has to answer before going to the bank. He earns some cash by helping out at Mom's office for a few hours on weekends. His responsibilities include jobs such as stuffing envelopes and watering the plants. Mom pays him $15 per week.

Today, Rob's parents are taking him to the bank to open a savings account. So far, he's earned $45 that he *could* deposit. Yet Rob isn't sure he wants to put all his money into savings. He occasionally needs cash to visit the mall or see a movie with his friends.

But Rob is planning ahead. In May, his favorite band is coming to town. The cheapest concert tickets cost $68.50 and go on sale in a month. Rob wants to be sure he's saved enough money by then to head straight to the box office.

To help Rob create a savings plan, Mom makes a suggestion. Her idea involves a ratio. Ratios show the relationships between the quantities, or amounts, of two or more items.

In this case, Rob's mom recommends the following ratio—$3 deposited for every $4 earned. **If he follows her advice, how much will he deposit today? In a month, will Rob have enough money in his account to pay for a concert ticket?**

DO THE MATH!

Let's say your job pays you $12.50 a week. You decide that each week, you'll deposit $5 for every $6 you earn. At the end of eight weeks, how much will you have deposited in the bank?

WHO'S BETTER AT BALANCING?

Gayle was elected treasurer of the student council last month! That means she'll keep track of the money the group spends and receives. She will work with Ms. Wilkes, the teacher who oversees the council, each month to look over the student council ledger. That's a record book that contains information about the group's finances.

Gayle writes an entry in the ledger whenever the council spends or earns money. She notes expenses in the column labeled "debits." Earnings are recorded in the column labeled "credits."

The balance is the money that remains after each entry. Gayle calculates the balance in the ledger by subtracting debits and adding credits. According to her, the current balance is $359.61.

Ms. Wilkes takes a quick peek at Gayle's work on the ledger sheet below. When she crunches the numbers, however, she gets a slightly different figure—$369.61.
Who's calculating the correct balance?

Date	Description	Debit ($)	Credit ($)	Balance ($)
sept. 1	starting balance for the month			193.56
sept. 5	New bulletin board to hang in the cafeteria	11.31		182.25
sept. 7	Back-to-school bake sale		112.10	284.35
sept. 14	240 buttons for school spirit week	26.25		258.10
sept. 15	Poster board (10-pack) for school spirit week decorations	6.99		251.11
sept. 19	Ticket sales from movie night		108.50	359.61
sept. 30	Ending balance for the month			359.61

A LITTLE LOAN

Splash! That's exactly the sound Saul hopes to hear soon. In six weeks, his local community center is sponsoring an overnight field trip to the Ocean Institute several hours away. Participants will get to study sea life with scientists and even explore the high-tech equipment they use! Saul is ready to sign up. First, however, he needs to figure out if he can afford it.

The institute charges a fee of $60 per person. And the director of the community center suggests that each participant bring about $25 in cash for snacks and meals during the long drives.

Saul's parents give him permission to go, but he'll have to pay 50 percent of the cost. If he needs to, he can borrow some extra money from Mom and Dad. Then Saul would hold off on collecting his allowance until he repays them. He usually gets a weekly allowance of $5.

So far, Saul has saved $7.50 in allowance money. **In six weeks, will Saul need to borrow money from his parents? If so, how many weeks should he plan on not receiving any allowance?**

DO THE MATH!

Let's say you want to go on the same field trip as Saul, and you're responsible for the full cost. You don't get an allowance, but you've recently received $45 in birthday money. Your grandparents also offer to help you earn extra cash raking leaves. Grandpa says he'll pay you $10 each time you clean up his yard. How many times will you need to rake to set aside enough money for the trip?

ADD CASH TO THE COOKIE JAR!

Anyone care for a cookie? How about a little cash instead? That's what Elle, Fay, George, and Jack put inside *their* cookie jar. They hope to eventually fill the jar with enough money to pay for a five-day, four-night vacation. Their family wants to rent a cottage near Lake Michigan. The rental rate is $290 per night.

There are no rules about how much everyone has to put in the cookie jar. Yet Elle, Fay, George, and Jack all plan to contribute some of their weekly allowance. They get 50¢ a week for each year of their age. Elle is nine, Fay is 12, George is 15, and Jack is 11. Fay also makes $15 a week working as a math tutor.

Mom and Dad agree to help, as well. They promise to match every dollar the kids save. To kick off the family savings plan, Dad drops $20 in the cookie jar on April 1.

For the next four weeks, money continues to pile up in place of cookies. Elle puts in her entire allowance during the first and third weeks of April. Fay contributes half of her total earnings. George gives $15. Finally, Jack adds $2.50 to the jar each week. **How much have the kids added to the jar at the end of four weeks? Once their parents match this amount, how much more will the family need?**

PICKING A PAYMENT PLAN

Wow, Bea always thought *she* was messy! Then she saw the closets and the basement at Aunt Jill's house. They're filled with thousands of photographs Aunt Jill has saved over the years. Some date back to Bea's great-grandparents! Written on the back of each one is the date the photo was taken.

Aunt Jill hasn't had time to get organized. So she asks Bea for help sorting all the pictures. Aunt Jill wants to arrange the photos in boxes, according to the date she took them.

It's a big job, so Aunt Jill offers Bea two payment options. The first involves a flat rate, or a single fixed fee, of $100. The second involves an hourly rate of $10.

Before choosing, Bea decides to figure out how much she can accomplish today. From 12:30 p.m. to 1:15 p.m., she gets busy. During that time, she sorts about half the photos in one closet.

Aunt Jill says there are about the same number of pictures in two other closets. She also warns that the basement is much bigger. Aunt Jill predicts it will be twice as much work as all three closets combined! **Based on what Bea's done so far—and what Aunt Jill's saying—which payment plan will earn Bea more?**

DO THE MATH!

Sometimes you help out in your aunt's greenhouse by planting seeds, watering flowers, and recording growth measurements. Your aunt pays you $9 an hour. You've been working at the greenhouse for a while, and she says you're doing great. So today, she's giving you a 3 percent raise! Spring break is coming up, and you'll be spending four days at her house. You plan to work in the greenhouse about two hours a day. How much money will you earn during spring break?

SELL FIRST, SHOP LATER!

Toys for sale! Dad always jokes that Abe has enough toys to open his own store. As Abe sets aside old toys for his family's garage sale, he realizes Dad is right!

Nowadays, Abe's plastic dinosaurs and superheroes don't get much use. Neither do his wooden blocks and teddy bears. Instead, Abe prefers to hang out with his friends, play sports, and read.

Coincidentally, Abe's favorite author just published two new graphic novels. The box set is $15.82. Abe can't wait to buy it, but he's short on cash.

Dad suggests that Abe use the money he makes at their upcoming garage sale. Dad says Abe can keep whatever money he earns from his old toys. This way, someone else will be able to enjoy Abe's toys. Plus, the house will be less cluttered. Abe likes Dad's plan and prices his toys as follows:

- Box of 28 wooden blocks—$7.50
- Teddy bears—$2 each
- Dinosaurs—25¢ each (or five for $1)
- Superheroes—75¢ each (or three for $2)

The day of the garage sale, Abe's first customer buys a teddy bear and two superheroes. Then a neighbor purchases 10 dinosaurs and one superhero. Abe sells a teddy bear and two dinosaurs to a third customer. Next, someone offers him $5 for the blocks. **If Abe accepts, will he have enough money to head to the bookstore?**

WHAT'S LEFT ON THE LUNCH CARD?

It's turkey burger day in the cafeteria! As Eve gets in line, she wonders about the balance on her lunch card. At Eve's school, lunch cards work like prepaid debit cards. At the beginning of the month, Mom writes a check for $25. The school loads the money onto Eve's card. Whenever she buys cafeteria food, she hands her card to the cashier.

If Eve brings her lunch, she only buys milk, which costs 45¢. If Eve buys a hot lunch, which includes milk, $2.90 is debited, or subtracted, from her card.

Eve hasn't remembered to check her balance during this month. Today is Wednesday, February 25. Eve knows that on Monday, February 2, $25 was added to her card. She also had $15.15 left from January.

Starting February 2, Eve has brought her lunch on Mondays and Fridays. (She still purchased milk on those days.) Eve has been buying hot lunch on Tuesdays, Wednesdays, and Thursdays. **Does Eve have enough money for hot lunch today and tomorrow?** (Hint: Refer to a calendar if you need to!)

DO THE MATH!

You and your brother also use prepaid lunch cards. Your school allows siblings to borrow money from each other's accounts. You bring your lunch Tuesdays and Thursdays but still buy milk those days. Your brother gets hot lunch every day. On Wednesday, February 25, your brother's card is out of money. You both need lunch today—on *your* card. The last time you checked your balance online was before school on Monday, February 9. Then you had $32.25 left. Is there currently enough on the card for both of you to have hot lunch?

A PIECE OF THE PIE

Whoa—trillions of dollars is a lot!

Wade is watching the news with Uncle Grant. The reporter is discussing the national budget. A budget is a type of financial plan. People create budgets to estimate earnings and expenses during a set period of time.

Wade is amazed by how big America's budget is. Suddenly, a pie chart pops up on the TV screen. Uncle Grant says it shows a breakdown of government expenses.

Studying this chart makes Wade think about *his* spending habits. Uncle Grant offers to help Wade get a better understanding of his budget. He suggests they make their own pie chart. This will help Wade visualize where his money's going.

They start by talking about his monthly earnings and expenses. Wade gets a monthly allowance of $27. The receipts in his wallet reveal how he spent his allowance last month.

Wade purchased a video game for $14.73 on June 3. On June 11 and 18, he got ice cream with his friends. It cost him $3.69 the first time and $4.09 the second time. The following week, Wade paid $6.25 for a movie ticket. He also spent $6.99 on a new shirt. Finally, Wade bought three cookies for $1 at the school bake sale.

First, Wade adds up all his expenses to figure out how much he spent altogether. Then Uncle Grant divides Wade's expenses into three categories—entertainment, food, and clothing. Next, Wade figures out how much of his total spending each category represents. Then he grabs markers to shade in a pie chart of his own. Blue = entertainment expenses, green = food expenses, and red = clothing expenses.

The percentage of Wade's total spending that each category represents = Wade's total spending in each category ÷ Wade's total expenses. **How much of the chart should he color blue? How about red and green?**

(Hint: Figure out how much of each color to use in the chart by converting each percentage to a fraction. Simply divide each fraction by 100. Your fractions should round into fifths, so divide your pie chart into five equal pieces.)

THE GIFT KEEPS ON GIVING

On Jade's fifth birthday, Grandma bought her a $75 savings bond. That's a type of certificate issued by the US government. When Grandma purchased the bond, she loaned the US government money in Jade's name. In turn, the government presented Jade with a bond as a promise of repayment—with interest. Interest is money a borrower pays to a lender for using the borrowed money.

The rate of interest is usually calculated as a percentage of the amount borrowed. The government pays a fixed, or set, rate of interest on certain bonds. Grandma says Jade's bond can earn interest for up to 30 years.

Yet Grandma purchased Jade's bond for half its face value, or the dollar amount printed on the front of a bond. And the bond earns interest on what Grandma paid. So it will take a while before it can be redeemed, or cashed in, for the face value.

Grandma explains that the interest is earned monthly but is only compounded twice a year. In other words, the bond earns interest every month. Yet, the sum of these earnings isn't added to the total value of the bond until the end of a six-month period. Then the set rate of interest is applied to that new total value. This process is repeated every six months.

Grandma bought Jade's bond five years ago. The fixed rate of interest was 1.4 percent. **If Jade cashes in the bond today, what will it be worth?** (Round to the nearest cent in all of these calculations.)

READY, SET, YOU'RE IN BUSINESS

So do you have any new ideas on what to do with the contents of that piggy bank? Perhaps you're thinking about spending it, saving it, or doing a little of each. Before you decide, solve a few final math problems involving money. As you calculate, maybe you'll figure out how to further improve your financial plan!

Are you ready to go into business? For sure! So are six of your friends. Together, the seven of you are working to get Handy Helpers off the ground. Handy Helpers will provide a variety of services including raking leaves, gardening, and shoveling snow. You're also happy to help with chores such as dog walking. Your parents will take turns chaperoning.

First, you and your pals decide to print fliers and use paint and poster board to create signs. You've already got computer paper, but you have to buy everything else. You agree to do the shopping, but everyone will ultimately split the overhead costs, or business expenses. At the office store, you spend $32.16. **How much does each of your friends owe you?**

Next, you set prices for the different services Handy Helpers will offer. You decide to charge $10 per hour for most lawn and gardening jobs. For dog walking, Handy Helpers' fee is $20 for four walks a week. The group votes to set aside 5 percent of any earnings toward future business expenses. Whatever is left over from a particular job will be divided evenly among whoever worked on it.

As your town learns about Handy Helpers, the company calendar begins to fill up. Right away, the business books three dog-walking gigs each week. You and your best friend split one of them. You're responsible for two walks a week. You and two other friends will also be raking leaves for a neighbor twice a month. You estimate that among the three of you, it should take about an hour and a half each time. **At the end of four weeks, how much money will you have made?**

Let's say you earn this same amount per week for the following two weeks (after the first four). Then, for three weeks, you need to focus on completing a big math project at school. During that period, you earn $7 less per week than usual. Nine weeks after you started working with Handy Helpers, you head to the bank. You've saved all your money so far. You plan to deposit $3 for every $5 you've earned. **How much will you add to your bank account?**

Answer Key

Page 5 Marge should expect to get $25 this month. ($3/yr. of Marge's age × 10 yrs. = $30/mo.; 5 ☻ this mo. = $5 deducted from Marge's allowance; $30/mo. – $5 = $25)

Do the Math!
Mom's plan is the better deal. (50¢ = $0.50; $0.50/yr. × 10 yrs. = $5/wk.; $5/wk. × 52 wks./yr. = $260/yr; $260/yr. ÷ 12 mos./yr. = $21.667/mo., or $21.67/mo. earned using Dad's plan; $21.67/mo. < $25/mo.; Mom's plan is the better deal.) That will change when you turn 12. Then you'd earn more on Dad's plan. (What you'd need to earn using Dad's suggested allowance plan to make his plan an equal or better deal must be ≥ $25/mo.; $25/mo. × 12 mo./yr. = $300/yr.; $300/yr. ÷ 52 wks./yr. = $5.769/wk., or $5.77/wk.; $5.77/wk. ÷ $0.50/yr. of your age = 11.54 yrs.; need age ≥ 11.54 for Dad's suggested allowance plan to be an equal or better deal; next birthday = 12))

Page 7 Joel should accept. ($10 + $15 + $20 = $45; $45 + $18.50 + $56 = $119.50; $119.50 < $149.95; $149.95 – $119.50 = $30.45 still needed)

Do the Math!
It will have to snow three times before you earn enough money for your skis. ($149.95 – $113.15 = $36.80 still needed; $36.80 ÷ $15 = 2.45, or 3 times shoveling)

Page 9 Bess should get $2.75. (3 12 fl. oz. cans × 5¢/container = 15¢; 15¢ = $0.15; $5.35 – $0.15 = $5.20; 50 percent = 0.50; $5.20 × 0.50 = $2.60; $2.60 + $0.15 = $2.75)

Page 11 If Rob follows Mom's advice, he will deposit $33.75 today. ($3 : $4 = ¾; ¾ × $45 = $33.75)
In a month, Rob will have enough money to pay for a concert ticket. ($15/wk. × 4 wks./mo. = $60; $60 × ¾ = $45; $45 + $33.75 = $78.75; $78.75 ≥ $68.50)

Do the Math!
At the end of eight weeks, you will have deposited $83.36 in the bank. ($5 : $6 = ⅚; ⅚ × $12.50 = $10.417, or $10.42 deposited each week; $10.42 × 8 = $83.36)

Page 13 Ms. Wilkes is calculating the correct balance. (Ms. Wilkes's calculations: Sept. 5: $193.56 – $11.31 = $182.25; Sept. 7: $182.25 + $112.10 = $294.35; Sept. 14: $294.35 – $26.25 = $268.10; Sept. 15: $268.10 – $6.99 = $261.11; Sept. 19: $261.11 + $108.50 = $369.61)

Page 15 Saul will need to borrow money from his parents. ($5/wk. × 6 wks. = $30; $30 + $7.50 = $37.50; $60/person + $25/person = $85/person; 50 percent = 0.50; 0.50 × $85/person = $42.50; $37.50 < $42.50)
Saul won't receive any allowance for one week after the trip. ($42.50 – $37.50 = $5; $5 ÷ $5/wk. = 1 wk.)

Do the Math
You'll need to rake four times. ($85/person – $45 = $40; $40 ÷ $10/raking = 4 rakings)

Page 17 At the end of four weeks, the kids have set aside $76. (Elle: 9 yrs. × $0.50/yr. = $4.50/wk.; 1st wk. + 3rd wk. = 2 wks.; 2 wks. × $4.50/wk. = $9; Fay: 12 yrs. × $0.50/yr. = $6/wk.; $6/wk. + $15/wk. = $21/wk.; $21/wk. × 4 wks. = $84; ½ × $84 = $42; George: $15; Jack: $2.50/wk. × 4 wks. = $10; $9 + $42 + $15 + $10 = $76) The family will still need $988. ($1 : $1 = ¼, or 1; 1 × $76 = $76; $76 + $76 + $20 = $172; $290/night × 4 nights = $1,160; $1,160 – $172 = $988)

Page 19 At the end of four weeks, the hourly rate is the better payment plan for Bea. (1:15 p.m. – 12:30 p.m. = 45 mins.; 45 mins. × 2 = 90 mins.; 90 mins. × 3 closets = 270 mins.; 270 mins. × 2 = 540 mins.; 270 mins. + 540 mins. = 810 mins.; 810 mins. ÷ 60 mins./hr. = 13.5 hrs.; 13.5 hrs. × $10/hr. = $135; $135 > $100)

Do the Math!
You'll earn $74.16 during spring break. (3 percent = 0.03; 0.03 × $9/hr. = $0.27/hr. raise; $9/hr. + $0.27/hr. = $9.27/hr.; 4 days × 2 hrs./day = 8 hrs.; $9.27/hr. × 8 hrs. = $74.16)

Page 21 If Abe accepts, he won't have enough money for the books. (75¢ = $0.75; $0.75/superhero × 2 superheroes = $1.50; $1.50 + $2 = $3.50 from first customer; $1/5 dinos × 10 dinos = $2 + $0.75 = $2.75 from second customer; 25¢ = $0.25; $0.25/dino × 2 dinos = $0.50; $0.50 + $2 = $2.50 from third customer; $3.50 + $2.75 + $2.50 + $5 = $13.75; $13.75 < $15.82)

Page 23 Eve has enough money to buy a hot lunch today and tomorrow. (Tues., Feb. 24 – Mon., Feb. 2 = 7 Mon. and Fri. + 10 Tues., Wed., and Thurs.; 7 Mon. and Fri. × $0.45/day = $3.15; 10 Tues., Wed., and Thurs. × $2.90/day = $29; $3.15 + $29 = $32.15; $15.15 + $25 = $40.15; $40.15 − $32.15 = $8.00 left on card; 2 days × $2.90/day = $5.80 needed for 2 lunches; $5.80 < $8.00)

Do the Math!
There is enough on the card for both of you to have hot lunch. (Tues., Feb. 24 – Mon., Feb. 9 = 5 Tues. and Thurs. + 7 Mon., Wed., and Fri.; 5 Tues. and Thurs. × $0.45/day = $2.25; 7 Mon., Wed., and Fri. × $2.90/day = $20.30; $2.25 + $20.30 = $22.55; $32.25 − $22.55 = $9.70; $2.90/day × 2 hot lunches = $5.80; $5.80 < $9.70)

Page 25 Wade should color ³/₅ of the chart blue. He should also color ¹/₅ of the chart green and ¹/₅ of the chart red. (Total expenses: $14.73 + $3.69 + $4.09 + $6.25 + $6.99 + $1 = $36.75; entertainment: $14.73 + $6.25 = $20.98; $20.98 ÷ $36.75 = 0.57, or 0.6; 0.6 = ⁶/₁₀, or ³/₅; food: $3.69 + $4.09 + $1 = $8.78; $8.78 ÷ $36.75 = 0.24, or 0.2; 0.2 = ²/₁₀, or ¹/₅; clothing: $6.99 ÷ $36.75 = 0.19, or 0.2; 0.2 = ²/₁₀, or ¹/₅)

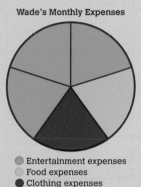

Wade's Monthly Expenses

● Entertainment expenses
● Food expenses
● Clothing expenses

Page 27 The bond would be worth $84.12 today. ($75 face value × ½ = $37.50; 5 yrs. × 12 mos./year = 60 mos.; 60 mos. ÷ 6 mos. per compounding time period = 10 time periods; 1.4 percent = 0.014; $37.50 paid for Jade's bond × 0.014 = $0.53/mo. interest during 1st 6 mos.; $0.53/mo. × 6 mos. = $3.18; $37.50 + $3.18 = $40.68 bond value after 1st 6 mos.; $40.68 × 0.014 = $0.57/mo. int. during 2nd 6 mos.; $0.57/mo. × 6 mos. = $3.42; $40.68 + $3.42 = $44.10 bond value after 2nd 6 mos.; $44.10 × 0.014 = $0.62/mo. int. during 3rd 6 mos.; $0.62/mo. × 6 mos. = $3.72; $44.10 + $3.72 = $47.82 bond value after 3rd 6 mos.; $47.82 × 0.014 = $0.67/mo. int. during 4th 6 mos.; $0.67/mo. × 6 mos. = $4.02; $47.82 + $4.02 = $51.84 bond value after 4th 6 mos.; $51.84 × 0.014 = $0.73/mo. int. during 5th 6 mos.; $0.73/mo. × 6 mos. = $4.38; $51.84 + $4.38 = $56.22 bond value after 5th 6 mos.; $56.22 × 0.014 = $0.79/mo. int. during 6th 6 mos.; $0.79/mo. × 6 mos. = $4.74; $56.22 + $4.74 = $60.96 bond value after 6th 6 mos.; $60.96 × 0.014 = $0.85/mo. int. during 7th 6 mos.; $0.85/mo. × 6 mos. = $5.10; $60.96 + $5.10 = $66.06 bond value after 7th 6 mos.; $66.06 × 0.014 = $0.92/mo. int. during 8th 6 mos.; $0.92/mo. × 6 mos. = $5.52; $66.06 + $5.52 = $71.58 bond value after 8th 6 mos.; $71.58 × 0.014 = $1.00/mo. int. during 9th 6 mos.; $1.00/mo. × 6 mos. = $6.00; $71.58 + $6.00 = $77.58 bond value after 9th 6 mos.; $77.58 × 0.014 = $1.09/mo. int. during 10th 6 mos.; $1.09/mo. × 6 mos. = $6.54; $77.58 + $6.54 = $84.12 bond value after 10th 6 mos.)

Pages 29 Each friend owes you $4.59. ($32.16 ÷ 7 friends = $4.594, or $4.59)
At the end of four weeks, you'll have made $57. (5 percent = 0.05; dog walking: $20/wk. × 0.05 = $1/wk. set aside; $20/wk. – $1/wk. = $19/wk. group income; $19/wk. ÷ 2 = $9.50/wk. each; $9.50/wk. × 4 wks. = $38; raking: 1½ hrs. = 1.5 hrs.; 1.5 hrs./wk. × $10/hr. = $15/wk.; $15/wk. × 0.05 = $0.75/wk. set aside; $15/wk. – $0.75/wk. = $14.25/wk. group income; $14.25/wk. ÷ 3 workers = $4.75/wk. each; $4.75/wk. × 4 wks. = $19; $38 + $19 = $57)
You'll add $64.35 to your bank account. ($57 ÷ 4 wks. = $14.25/wk. during wks. 1–6; $14.25/wk. – $7/wk. = $7.25/wk. during wks. 7–9; $14.25/wk. × 6 wks. = $85.50; $7.25/wk. × 3 wks. = $21.75; $85.50 + 21.75 = $107.25; $3 : $5 = ³/₅; ³/₅ × $107.25 = $64.35)

Glossary

aluminum: a silvery-gray recyclable material that's often used to make beverage containers

compound: to calculate interest on a sum that includes previously earned interest

credit: a sum that has been earned or received

debit: a sum that has been deducted or is owed

debit card: a card that allows someone to transfer money electronically to make a purchase

deduct: to subtract a certain amount from a larger total sum

deposit: to place money in a bank account

estimate: to calculate without using precise numbers or information

predict: to declare that something will happen or is likely to happen in the future

rate: a fixed price paid or charged for something, especially goods or services

Further Information

IXL Learning: Third Grade
http://www.ixl.com/math/grade-3
This site provides examples and practice problems to help you perfect your growing math skills.

Kemper, Bitsy. *Budgeting, Spending, and Saving.* Minneapolis: Lerner Publications, 2015. Figure out fun and clever ways to build your own budget and spend money wisely.

Marsico, Katie. *Shopping Trip Math.* Minneapolis: Lerner Publications, 2015. Explore additional opportunities to test your knowledge of both money and math.

TheMint.org—Fun for Kids
http://www.themint.org/kids/
This site offers tips and suggestions for earning, spending, and saving money responsibly.

Index